Mystery Sea Serpents

of the South-West

Chris

Bossiney Books • Launceston

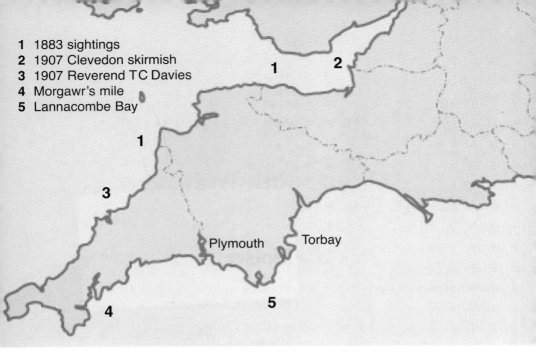

1 1883 sightings
2 1907 Clevedon skirmish
3 1907 Reverend TC Davies
4 Morgawr's mile
5 Lannacombe Bay

Key areas for sea serpent sightings in Cornwall, Devon and Somerset

Also by Chris Moiser:
Mystery Cats of the South-West

First published 2004 by Bossiney Books Ltd
Langore, Launceston, Cornwall PL15 8LD
www.bossineybooks.co.uk
Copyright © 2004 Chris Moiser   All rights reserved
ISBN 1-899383-68-9
Cover illustration and map by Nick Hawken
Other illustrations are from the *Strand* magazine, 1895
Printed in Great Britain by Short Run Press Ltd, Exeter

Introduction

Cryptozoology is the word used to describe the study of strange and mystery animals or, if literally translated from the Greek, the study of hidden or secret animals.

There is an almost unspoken rule that cryptozoologists only really look at species not known to, or accepted by, science.

In the world of cryptozoology one often finds that words and phrases take on slightly different meanings from those normally attributed to them. This has been particularly true with the term 'sea serpent' which has been extended far beyond large snake-like animals. It is now generally accepted that the term covers a whole range of monsters that live in the sea. Whether they have limbs, fins, hair or antennae seems irrelevant; if they are large unknown animals seen in the oceans they are 'sea serpents'. For the purist who thinks the term 'serpent' should be restricted to snake-like animals it is of course still acceptable to refer to 'sea monsters' or even 'unknown sea animals'.

It is difficult not to start a book on sea serpents without referring to possibly the oldest reference to such an animal, which appears in the Bible:

> and he shall slay the dragon that is in the sea
>
> *Isaiah* (27:1)

Whilst this does not help in tracing sea serpent activity in Devon, Cornwall and Somerset it does perhaps indicate a long history of the possible existence of such animals. The full Isaiah reference carefully lists the dragon as separate from two types of serpent. What is not clear is which sea is referred to, but it would seem safe to presume that it is the Mediterranean. This suggests the dragon could have been the Nile Crocodile, an animal which can reach 5 metres in length, will swim in sea water and was present in the Nile delta until the 1700s. Crocodiles are survivors from an ancient line of animals and often surprise us by having survived in unlikely circumstances if you consider their currently much reduced aquatic tropical habitats.

Dragons are frequently referred to in West Country folklore, but these are unlikely to be crocodiles, and are far too terrestrial in most accounts to be confused with the sea serpents, which are generally wholly aquatic entities.

Sea serpent attacking a ship, from an edition of Olaus Magnus. It was reported to be 200 ft (60 m) long and 20 ft (6 m) in girth, with fiery eyes and a short mane

Reports of sea serpents in post-biblical times were recorded fairly regularly from the 1550s onwards. Many of the earliest ones come from the coast of Norway and are contained in the writings of Olaus Magnus, the Archbishop of Uppsala.

During the sixteenth to eighteenth centuries most of the sea serpent records were made in the general area of Scandinavia and appear to have been prepared by clerics following in the footsteps of Olaus Magnus. The number of sightings built to a peak, with the nineteenth century having the most reports. This does not necessarily mean the sea serpents of the time had a greater wish to be seen! It may have been the result of a great many ships at sea, often travelling large distances at relatively low speeds, and the keenness of the newspapers to report matters of strangeness.

Possibly the best known sighting of the nineteenth century, and the one taken most seriously, was that made from HMS *Daedalus* on 6 August 1848. It virtually set the standards for future sightings and, because of the reliability of the witnesses (Royal Naval officers), made a mythical animal into a real one for most ordinary folk.

Although the sea serpent, an animal estimated to be one hundred feet long, was viewed for twenty minutes as the ship sailed between the Cape of Good Hope and the island of St Helena, there is a South West connection. The story first became public when the ship arrived back at Plymouth. She docked on 4 October 1848, and the first report of the sea serpent appeared in *The Times* on 9 October. So astounding was this report that the Admiralty immediately inquired into the details. To his credit, the captain, Peter M'Quhae, responded quickly, both to the Lords Commissioners of the Admiralty and to *The Times*.

Most of the crew were at supper when the animal was first seen by Mr Sartoris, a midshipman. He then reported it to the officer of the watch, Lieutenant Drummond, who drew it to the captain's attention. The quartermaster, the boatswain's mate and the 'man at the wheel' also saw the animal. The captain described it as being an enormous serpent with a head about four feet above the surface of the sea and a body at least sixty feet long on the surface and fifteen or sixteen inches in diameter. There were no visible fins. Something of a mane, like that of a horse, or a bunch of seaweed, also 'washed around its back'.

The animal was dark brown in colour with a yellowish white around the throat. Sketches were subsequently produced, as was a

Hans Egede, a missionary on his way to Greenland, apparently saw this creature in 1734

The sighting by HMS Daedalus, *1848*

report by Lieutenant Drummond which was entirely consistent with the captain's.

Much correspondence about the sighting appeared throughout the rest of the year. Some people acknowledged its uniqueness, others suggested it was a misidentification of animals already known to science. One particular disbeliever was Professor Richard Owen, the inventor of the word 'dinosaur', and a well-known zoologist. Captain M'Quhae and his officers stuck to their original story.

The return of HMS *Daedalus* to Plymouth was also notable for other reasons: the ship was returning from the Far East and brought with it a collection of Chinese art which was exhibited at the Royal William Yard, Plymouth, for a few days. She also carried a black leopard and a tree kangaroo which were gifts from the Governor of Singapore to the Zoological Society of London. The tree kangaroo was apparently the first living specimen of its kind to reach England.

Whilst the '*Daedalus* sea serpent' was not, in any sense, formal proof of the existence of large, previously unknown sea monsters, it added considerably to the credibility of earlier reported sightings, and made people in the future less reluctant to report sightings for fear of ridicule.

The Royal Navy came up with another sighting very quickly. An officer on board HMS *Plumper* wrote to the editor of the *Illustrated*

London News on 10 April 1849, claiming to have seen a large sea serpent due west of Oporto on New Year's Eve 1848. Although the officer's name was never published and the report of the sea serpent does not appear in the ship's log, the ship's position was as suggested in the newspaper report. In addition the officer had supplied a sketch of the sea serpent which showed a similar animal to that drawn by the crew member of the *Daedalus*. Another sea serpent sighting was reported in 1849 by HMS *Cleopatra*; this time from the Indian Ocean.

If the descriptions noted by HMS *Plumper* and HMS *Daedalus* are accurate, they represent animals which are still unknown to science, and indeed which may, sadly, have gone extinct in the meantime. Some sea serpents of course are easily identified, but in terms of size alone they are still 'monsters' and will impress those lucky enough to see them. Possibly the earliest record of a proven real 'sea monster' I have found in the South West is that of a whale which was washed ashore on the western side of Penlee Point, six miles from Plymouth, on or about 12 January 1781.

The following Friday the *Exeter Flying Post* carried a detailed report of the animal which was seventy feet long, with a tail fifteen feet wide. From the description it was clearly a baleen whale, that is a whale which filters sea water to extract microscopic food. The report suggested it was 'a fin fish', and the description and size are certainly consistent with it being a Fin Whale (*Balaenoptera physalus*), the second largest species of whale. Its size, if accurate, really excludes it from being anything else.

The interest it evoked at the time was quite amazing, with the Lord of the Manor placing a guard on the body to protect it from those who went to view it. The Mutton Cove ferry dock was said to be like a fair and people waded out to the ferry up to their waists in cold January waters to be sure of crossing on the next trip to see the animal.

Sea serpent attacking a sperm whale, as reported by Captain Drevar of the barque Pauline, *on 8 July 1875. He and his crew made a declaration before a magistrate in Liverpool that 'The serpent whirled its victim round and round for about fifteen minutes, and then suddenly dragged the whole to the bottom, head first.'*

Other nineteenth-century serpents

Although there are numerous reports of sea serpent sightings from around the world during the nineteenth century, there are very few from the South West coast. However in 1875 *The West Briton* newspaper reported a sea serpent having been captured at Portscatho in Cornwall. It was found 400 yards offshore coiled around the buoy which was attached to some crab pots. As it lifted its head towards the fishermen who approached it, and 'showed signs of defiance', it was struck with an oar and 'disabled'. It was later brought ashore and shown to the locals before being killed on the rocks and thrown back into the sea.

On the afternoon of 11 October 1883 Reverend Highton, the vicar of Bude in Cornwall, along with several friends saw a sea serpent about a mile and a half off the Bude coast. He described it as a long, low dark object, skimming along the surface of the sea at about twenty-five miles per hour. It was viewed for around ten minutes and those present estimated its length as between fifty and eighty feet. Interestingly, many books report this incident as having happened on 11 October 1882 and having been reported in *The Times* on the 12th. It was actually published on 17 October 1883. Finding the original report took considerable time for this reason, and would not have been possible without the help of *The Times* record office.

Another report in October 1883, this time in a paper called *The*

Graphic, states, almost with a degree of tedium, 'The inevitable sea-serpent has turned up again. This time he has been seen going down the Bristol Channel towards the Atlantic at the rate of twenty-five miles per hour, and afterwards he was noticed off the North coast of Cornwall. The monster was about half a mile long, and left a greasy trail behind him.'

Quite coincidentally a letter from Vice Admiral Gore-Jones appeared in *The Times* on the same day as the account in *The Graphic*. Gore-Jones, clearly a non-believer, recounted a tale from his past when as a junior officer in 1848 he was on HMS *St Vincent* at Spithead. It was a warm summer evening shortly after the *Daedalus* sea serpent report had been published and the officers were just sitting down to dinner. The midshipman of the watch dashed in to say that a sea serpent was passing between the ship and the Isle of Wight.

Dinner was abandoned and some of the more intrepid officers set off in the boats with their guns, whilst the others watched from the deck. As the boats approached the monster there was suddenly great hilarity when it was realised that the 'monster' was a long line of soot. As Gore-Jones was keen to point out, had the boats not been launched the entire crew would have believed they had seen a hundred foot long sea serpent.

Early twentieth-century serpents

Whilst the number of reported sea serpent sightings in the South West during the nineteenth century were few, the same cannot be said of the early twentieth century. In August 1906 the American liner *St Andrew* was passing Land's End when one of the passengers saw a strange animal break the surface. It was 'serpent-like' with a body five feet in circumference. At one stage it was supposed to have raised its head clear of the water to display a set of powerful jaws with great 'fin-like' teeth. Two of the ship's officers saw the animal before it dived. One of them, the first officer, asked the witness not to mention it to the other passengers in case it made them nervous.

In 1907 there were a number of sightings in the region. One of the first of note was reported as what might have been described as the 'Clevedon skirmish'. A Scottish visitor to the town, a Mr McNaughton, was rowing a small boat about one mile offshore when he was approached by a long snake-like animal 'like a huge mummy with sunken eyes...' that somehow knocked him into the sea. He was apparently able to climb back into the boat and, somewhat surprisingly, continued on his way to Portishead, several miles distant! For some reason this report appeared in the *Liverpool Echo* of 30 April 1907, the incident allegedly having happened on the previous Sunday.

In early September the same year a much more believable sighting occurred on the north Cornish coast. The reverend T C Davies and Mr Edward Dodgson of Jesus College, Oxford, were sitting on the edge of the cliffs at Tintagel when they saw a sea serpent about twenty feet long, with its head held aloft, moving rapidly about 200 yards away from them. The head apparently had some type of mane or crest. Neither of the observers had a telescope, 'still less a kodak [camera]', so no further detail was possible. Their sighting was made at 11.45 am on a Thursday morning in good visibility.

Further corroboration came two days later with a letter in the *Western Morning News* (16 September 1907) from Miss Mason, who, with a friend, had seen the animal at the same time but from a different part of the cliffs. Miss Mason and the two gentlemen were apparently unacquainted. A second letter published on the same day from T V Hodgson of the Plymouth Museum and Art Gallery suggested that the animal sighted might have been a ribbon or oar fish. Mr Hodgson stated, quite correctly, that these reach a length of around twenty feet plus, and that twenty-five or more had already been caught from the British coast.

At some unspecified time in 1907, a further sighting of a sea serpent off the coast at Padstow in north Cornwall was made by Mrs Adkins and her cousin. The animal had a long neck and was described as moving very lazily across the bay towards the Camel river. Unfortunately the girls were ridiculed when they first reported the sighting, and it was only following an article in *The Times* in late 1933 that Mrs Adkins felt able to describe the sighting to the media.

Another north coast sighting, this time off the Devon coast, happened in 1911, when William Cook was rowing three ladies from Instow to Westward Ho! At one stage of the journey he altered his course to avoid what he thought were rocks. But the rocks moved and started to lash the water, so he headed straight for the shore as a matter of safety. Without the head becoming visible he estimated the body to be between sixty and ninety feet long and the width of a barrel. It was greyish brown with scales, and the animal had an interrupted black dorsal fin which seemed to run virtually the full length of the visible body.

On 5 July 1912 Captain Ruser of the Hamburg-America line ship *Kaiserin Augusta Victoria* saw a twenty foot long, eighteen inch thick eel-like creature thrashing about at the water surface off Prawle Point, near to Salcombe on the south Devon coast. Visibility was good and the animal was blue-grey on its back and white on the underside. The details were recorded in the ship's log, and despite the ship being a fairly large liner it is perhaps understandable that no passengers saw the animal when it is realised the sighting was recorded at 06.35.

Sea serpents at war

There are two war incidents which have been commonly reported in articles and books on sea serpents. Both concern German U-boats during the First World War, and both have proved difficult to research back as far as the original documents. Interestingly, they occurred broadly speaking in the South West of England, one off the south coast, the other, loosely, off the north coast. (A third incident was also reported as taking place during World War I, but this possibly was in the North Sea, and the reports contain several contradictions.)

The first incident involves the sinking of the British steamer *Iberian* (5223 tons) by the U 28. On the evening of 30 July 1915 the U 28 was on patrol in the Atlantic, between North Devon and the Irish Republic, near Fastnet, when the *Iberian* was sighted. The submarine put itself into an attack position and engaged the *Iberian* with torpedoes. The steamer sank quickly and about 25 seconds later there was a massive explosion under water. A few seconds afterwards pieces of wreckage and a giant sea animal were blown out of the water to a height of sixty to one hundred feet.

The animal was described as unlike anything the conning tower crew had ever seen before. It was around sixty feet long, crocodile-like in shape and had four limbs with webbed feet and a long tail tapering to a point. It was writhing and struggling wildly and sank out of sight after 10 or 15 seconds before the crew could photograph it.

Altogether the captain, Kapitän-leutnant Georg-Gunther von

Forstner, and five crew saw the creature, and the engineer later made a rough sketch of it.

Despite this sighting occurring in 1915 it was 1933 before the details became public knowledge. Just after some Loch Ness monster sightings had been reported, the captain described what he had seen during the war in the German newspaper, *Deutsche Allgemeine Zeitung.*

Two years later the U 28 submarine, then under Kapitän-leutnant Georg Schmidt, was sunk in strange circumstances of her own making when she attacked the British steamer *Olive Branch* off North Cape in the Arctic Ocean. The U 28 attacked the steamer and the crew abandoned ship but the steamer remained afloat. The submarine then closed in to sink the ship with gunfire.

Unfortunately she came too close and when the munitions in the hold detonated there was a massive explosion which projected a lorry, being carried as deck cargo, upward to a great height. The lorry fell back down, landing on the U 28 at about the same time as the shock wave from the explosion hit the submarine. It is not known whether the submarine's hull was breached or whether she was swamped by flooding through open hatches, but the result was that she sank without survivors – a loss of 39 lives and the first submarine to be sunk by a lorry! The crew of *Olive Branch* survived.

The second incident is definitely nearer home and concerns the sinking of the German submarine U 85. The official record of the wreck states that the circumstances of the sinking of the U 85 are unknown, other than that she was sunk by gunfire from HMS *Privet.* HMS *Privet* was a decoy ship or Q boat, operating as Q 19.

The U 85 was sunk on 12 March 1917 and rests 25 miles SSE off Start Point in about 68 metres of water. These facts are certain; what is less certain is what caused this submarine to be on the surface in daylight. Normally submarines remained submerged during the day and surfaced at night to recharge their batteries and for general ventilation.

Some of the books on sea serpents say that the submarine was on the surface during daylight hours because she was damaged at night, and was subsequently unable to dive at daybreak. The damage was allegedly caused when a large animal suddenly climbed aboard causing the boat to list to starboard. It then gripped the forward gun mount. The animal was said to have large eyes set in a horny type of skull, and teeth that gleamed in the moonlight.

The crew on watch fired at it with sidearms but it held on for some time. When it finally let go and slipped back into the sea they discovered it had buckled some forward deck plates and the submarine was no longer able to submerge. The only problem with this is that the official report states that all hands on board were lost. If this was so, how did the sea serpent attack get reported?

Recent research into records at the Royal Submarine Museum at Gosport effectively destroy the sea serpent attack story by clarifying what happened. The U 85 attacked the Q ship whilst submerged, using a torpedo. The torpedo passed under the *Privet,* and in order to conserve her torpedoes for attacking bigger ships, the U 85 surfaced and attempted to sink the *Privet* by gunfire. After several direct hits, the *Privet* revealed her guns, engaged the U 85 and eventually sank her. There were no survivors.

There is further confusion about this report because of the submarine's number, U 85; the UB 85 was also sunk, just over a year later, off the Irish coast. At least one sea serpent report has relocated the captain of the UB 85, Kapitän Krech, to the U 85. The captain of the U 85 at the time she was sunk, however, was Willy Petz. A further mystery exists in that in the Second World War another U 85 was also sunk, this time off the American coast, under circumstances which indicated a clandestine operation.

The third and final incident during the First World War involved another U-boat which reported a similar sea serpent to that seen by the U 28. Werner Löwisch was a watch officer on the U 108 in the North Atlantic. One night at 10 pm he noticed a 'sea serpent… without any possibility of doubt, the creature had a longish head, scales like a crocodile, and legs with proper feet.' Apparently the mate also saw the animal which was about ninety feet long, but it had vanished by the time the captain arrived on deck.

This report, with a number of variations, has been recorded in several books. One places the U-boat in the North Sea when Löwisch saw his sea serpent and gives the date of 28 July 1918. It also identifies the U-boat as the U 109. This is clearly inaccurate, as the U 109 sank with the loss of all hands on 26 January 1918. Another report suggests that Löwisch was on the U 20 when the sea serpent was sighted. This would contradict the alleged sighting being in 1918, since the U 20 was blown up in 1916 by her own crew who had run her aground on the Danish coast. There is no evidence of Löwisch having served on the U 20, whose main claim to fame was sinking the RMS *Lusitania* in 1915. If this encounter happened in July 1918 it would seem it must have been the U 108 that was involved.

Between the wars

In the immediate post-war period there were few, if any sea serpent sightings reported in the South West of England. However they started again in 1926 with a very close encounter for two Cornish fishermen who were trawling three miles south of Falmouth. Mr Reese and Mr Gilbert caught a twenty foot long creature in their nets. It had an eight foot tail, a beak two feet long and six inches wide, and four scaly legs. The flat, wide back was covered in matted brown hair. Unfortunately it escaped, tearing the nets as it did so, but it did leave behind some blood and hair. It was reported that the fishermen took the hair to the Plymouth Marine Biological Observatory (now the Marine Biological Association), but they were unable to offer any opinion on it.

Another body turned up in the late 1920s, though it remained unreported for a few years until one of the witnesses wrote to *The Times*. The find was at Praa Sands (in Mount's Bay, south-west Cornwall) in spring 1928 and was of a headless animal whose body was about thirty feet long and four feet in diameter at its greatest width. It also had four feet-like flippers and a long tapering tail. The witness, Mr Garmesan, was not able to photograph the remains.

It is possibly worth pointing out that, whilst his description suggests a body form which is similar to a plesiosaur, another set of body remains recovered in 1977 by the Japanese trawler *Zuiyo-maru* turned out to be a partly decomposed shark. The typical pattern of decomposition of a shark is such that the gills and lower jaw decay first and drop away, leaving the 'narrow neck' linking the remains of the head to the rest of the body. This does look plesiosaur-like.

The 1930s started quietly but then came an absolute avalanche of reports, not just from the South West of England, but worldwide. This may have been prompted in part by the publicity given to a plethora

14

of sightings of the 'monster' at Loch Ness, which were reported in December 1933 following the publication of the report on the evidence gathered by Lieutenant-Commander Gould.

More reports followed during the mid 1930s. In fact it was only as a result of Lieutenant-Commander Gould's report that Mr Garmesan bothered to describe his discovery on Praa Sands in 1928.

A surprise finding in late 1933, though, could not be blamed on the Loch Ness monster. The *Western Morning News* of Saturday 23 December 1933 carried a photograph showing two local boys, Patrick Timmins and Jack White, holding between them a dead crocodile, approximately two to three feet in length. The accompanying report stated that they had found the animal, already dead, on rocks near the South Western Yacht Club, in Plymouth, the previous day.

They took it to the Marine Biological Association where an expert identified it as a young crocodile, possibly from the Mediterranean. There was a suggestion that it had been brought back to the UK by a sailor and had either died or been thrown overboard alive and succumbed to the cold when the sailor realised there would be a problem in landing it. The latter explanation seems quite likely, and it is possible the animal had indeed been taken on board a ship in the Mediterranean. Although the Nile crocodile was already extinct on the Mediterranean coast by then, the animals were occasionally still being sold in the tourist markets in Egypt.

Nile crocodiles can tolerate salt water to some extent, and they are sometimes found at sea off the Kenyan coast. It is perhaps also worth mentioning that a 'large alligator' was reportedly captured by the crew of a Dutch fishing boat off Orfordness (Suffolk) in 1833. It was said to be exhausted, but alive. Whilst British waters might be too cold for any of the crocodiles in the long term it should be borne in mind that the American alligator may be found in climates that can really only be described as temperate, and that a relict population of Nile crocodiles has recently been found at 400 metres above sea level in Mauritania – a place where the nights can be very cool.

The South West sightings of more mysterious sea serpents began again in May 1935. Port Isaac bay produced the first major sighting, with four people seeing a large black creature with a 'goose-like neck, a humped back and a tremendous tail'. It was between thirty and forty feet long and at one stage came so close to land that Mr Honey, a local

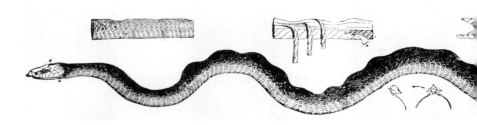

*Claimed as a sea serpent, this creature was apparently caught in 1817
in the harbour of Gloucester, Mass., and dissected by the Linnaean
Society of Boston, who were satisfied it was a young sea serpent*

postman, told a representative of the *Western Morning News* that one
could have jumped on to its back from the edge of Castle Rock. Over
the next few days the local fishermen all searched for the animal but
without success.

Two weeks later the *Western Morning News* carried a report of a
sighting at Stoke Beach, Revelstoke, near Plymouth. This animal was
much smaller, being about seven feet long and described as having a
head like a calf. Its skin was scaly according to one witness, but this
same witness then suggested it looked like a whale (which of course
does not have scales). The staff at the Marine Biological Laboratory in
Plymouth were inclined to think it might have been a basking shark
or a thresher shark, and the Yealm Coastguard suggested it might have
been a porpoise as several had been seen in the area recently.

There were a number of sightings off the south Devon coast the following year, this time starting at Brixham in early August when two
visitors spotted an animal said to be travelling at sixty miles per hour
off Sharkham Point. It was sixty to ninety feet long and had irregular
humps or fins. Two weeks later, on 24 August, a Noss Mayo resident,
Mrs A C Harrison, saw a smaller animal 'over thirty feet' long at the
entrance to Plymouth Sound. She was first drawn to looking at it
because of the cries of gulls nearby, and she described it as a 'very dark
mass' under water, which then came to the surface. This time, when
asked for a comment, the Marine Biological Association suggested it
'might have been a basking shark or, more probably, "holiday imagi-
nation"'.

The following day the *Western Morning News* carried another

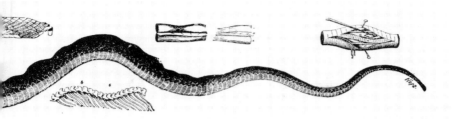

report about a possible sea monster that one of its readers from Plymouth had made. This animal had been seen about two weeks previously, in the Sound, by the reader whilst she was on her way to Jennycliff.

What neither of these reports mentioned, but is evident from articles elsewhere in the newspapers, was that the area was in the middle of a heatwave. There were very stable sea conditions and thousands of pilchards were being caught in Plymouth Sound. Such conditions would of course have been conducive for basking sharks, but they could also have attracted large marine predators.

The Second World War to the 1970s

As far as reports of sightings of sea serpents during the Second World War are concerned the situation is simple: there weren't any in the South West of England! Even on an international basis there were very few. Bernard Heuvelmans in his great 1965 textbook lists only nine sightings worldwide during this time.

The post-war period was initially very quiet, but then came a report of an extraordinary sighting. On 5 July 1949 Harold Wilkins and a friend were on the coastal waters near East Looe when, near midday, they saw 'two remarkable saurians'. These animals were described as fifteen to twenty feet long with bottle-green heads. They were mostly submerged, but the dorsal parts that were visible were ridged and serrated 'like the old Chinese pictures of dragons'. The animals were apparently chasing a shoal of fish up the tidal creek of East Looe. This is quite astonishing, as it would place them in the middle of a busy fishing port. However, no other sightings were reported. Wilkins was in no doubt that these animals were not of any kind currently known to be extant, and he clearly stated: 'These monsters – and two of us saw them – resembled the plesiosaurus of Mesozoic times'.

I might be called cynical for pointing out that Wilkins had already written such classic books as *Mysteries of the Great War* (which described some of the sea serpent–U-boat encounters) and was later to write *Monsters and Mysteries*. His sighting might be described as 'convenient', although if it was indeed genuine it may have stimulated him to write some of his later books.

The next few years were again very quiet, with no sightings reported in Cornwall, Devon or Somerset. There was a twenty-eight foot long 'blob' washed up on the beach between Tregantle and Port Wrinkle in September 1967, but this turned out to be decomposing whale blubber.

The early 1970s brought a series of reports from south Devon, but few sightings. Most of the early ones concerned divers hearing what they described as a 'fiendish bark' whilst submerged. On 17 August 1970 the *Western Morning News* reported that Graham Sampson, a skin diver from Kingsbridge, described having heard the bark at a depth of eighty feet. Subsequent discussion with fellow divers revealed that at least four of them had heard similar noises within the previous few weeks.

The phenomenon became known as 'the Lannacombe Bark' because it had been encountered just off the coast of this Devonshire hamlet. At about the same time the Salcombe Shark Angling Society had members claiming they were hooking what they presumed to be a fish, in mid-channel, which they played for a time and then lost. When they reeled in their lines the hooks were bitten through. It was thought that none of the sharks found in British waters could do this.

By October there were suggestions that the animal responsible could be a giant conger eel. The Torbay branch of the British Sub-Aqua Club suggested it could have been an eel that one of their members had seen and estimated to be over 120 pounds (55 kilos) in weight and eight foot in length. Other members of the club had seen a similar eel, and often at about the depth of eighty feet, but had given it a wide berth. There was even speculation that the animal might live in a rock formation about one mile off Lannacombe.

Half way through the following year there was further speculation within the area when both locals and tourists reported seeing the head of an animal above the surface on numerous occasions between Start

Point and Lannacombe Bay. Several of these witnesses put the body size at twenty feet in length and were of the opinion that it was too big to be a conger eel.

Interestingly, there had been sightings of strange marine animals in the Lannacombe Bay area since 1906. When a yachtsman called Mr Butler had watched as a buff-coloured 'baby monster' wriggled past his dinghy. It was only six feet long, and the description was similar to that of a ribbon fish. The 1912 sighting of the twenty foot long eel-like creature from the German ship *Kaiserin Augusta Victoria* off Prawle Point was only a few miles away.

Morgawr

If any sea serpent can claim to be associated with the South West it must be 'Morgawr'. Morgawr literally translated from the Cornish means 'sea giant'. It has only really appeared in the press since 1975, despite sea serpent sightings having been recorded from both the north and south coast of Cornwall for over a hundred years.

Typically the sightings of Morgawr occurred from the 1970s onwards and were in the Helford estuary, with the majority being between Toll Point and Rosemullion Head. This area is now some-times called 'Morgawr's mile' for this reason. The first of the modern sightings of note occurred a few miles to the east of Morgawr's mile, off Pendennis Point, in September 1975. Mrs Scott, of Falmouth, and her friend Mr Riley saw 'a hideous hump-backed creature, with stumpy horns, and bristles down the back of its neck'. This large ani-mal apparently dived below the surface and subsequently reappeared with a conger eel in its mouth.

The story certainly continued at a pace in 1976. In January a strange body was discovered on Durgan Beach by Mrs Payne of Falmouth. Sadly this body was never professionally examined and its identity has remained a mystery to this day. Earlier in the same month Duncan Viner, a dental technician from Truro, saw an animal that he first thought to be a whale swimming off Rosemullion Head. When he watched a long neck rise up from the water though, he realised that it was not a whale. Long necks, as an anatomical feature, are about as unwhale-like as it is possible to get. This animal was estimated to have been thirty to forty feet long.

In March the *Falmouth Packet* published two photographs of Morgawr which were allegedly taken in February at Trefusis Point near Flushing by 'Mary F' of Falmouth. Subsequent investigations failed to find Mary F. The article, however, did encourage further correspondence, including reports of eye witness accounts. In later years it was suggested that 'Mary F' was a nom-de-plume for a friend of Doc Shiels. Tony 'Doc' Shiels is a professional wizard and 'psychic' who at that time had attracted a good deal of publicity with various antics; despite this he impressed many contemporary investigators with his obviously genuine interest in strange phenomena.

Further sightings in the early part of the year described the animal as 'a sort of prehistoric dinosaur thing with a neck the length of a lamp-post', and 'slimy, black and about twenty five feet long'.

A fake monster also made an appearance in the Penryn River, but that was for an April 1st prank. On this occasion it was a twenty foot long, three humped red and green monster that followed very closely behind a local trawler.

In May two London bankers, apparently unaware of the monster stories, were fishing from the rocks near Parson's Beach when a greeny-grey body was spotted out of the water between one hundred and two hundred yards away. 'It' looked at them for ten seconds or so and then disappeared.

It was in July 1976 that Tony 'Doc' Shiels became publicly involved. He and his family were enjoying the hot weather on Grebe Beach when he saw 'a large, dark, long-necked, hump-backed beast moving slowly through the water'. Doc Shiels's sightings were bound to arouse suspicion: he had already had articles published by *Fortean Times*, the magazine of strange phenomena, and he was effectively working in the media. On 17 November 1976 at Mawnan, on the Helford River, he had a meeting with David Clarke, a journalist from the magazine *Cornish Life*.

The objective of this meeting was to take photographs of Shiels invoking the monster by magical means. But things were somewhat disturbed by the arrival of an animal head half way across the river. At first it was thought to be that of a seal but, as it moved nearer, Clarke noticed the head was supported by a long arched neck, narrower than that of a seal. This neck was four or five feet long in the troughs of the waves. The head was a greenish-brown and rounded with a blunt nose and two small rounded bumps on top.

After Clarke's dog barked, the head dived and was not seen again. Although both men tried to photograph the animal, neither was successful in doing so, Clarke's pictures being multiply exposed, and Shiels's camera having only a 'standard lens' which produced a print showing a very small head surrounded by a great deal of sea.

Clarke later published a full account of the meeting in the January 1977 issue of *Cornish Life* and admitted that he had considered trickery but could not see how it could have been done. Additionally he reported that after the incident both men had gone to the Red Lion pub in Mawnan Smith where they had recounted their experiences to a group of customers. The customers had heard of a number of sightings up the river at Durgan, but none had heard of any sightings locally. Clarke was convinced he had seen something, but was not willing to commit himself to say exactly what it was.

One of the best sightings from the summer of 1976 was by Cornish fishermen George Vinnicombe and John Cock who saw the animal twenty-five miles south of the Lizard. They chanced upon what looked like a huge 'tyre' about four feet out of the water. As they approached, its head – like 'an enormous seal' – rose up, the animal looked at them and then submerged. The body, about twenty-two feet in total length, was black, and the head was grey.

Sightings continued on a regular basis over the next few years. In May 1977 a particularly strange event happened when a couple from Plymstock were walking along Pendennis Point when they witnessed a bright orange ball in the sky with green flames coming from it. An hour later, on the same walk, they then saw a large dark creature heading out to sea. No further identification was possible, but both felt that it wasn't anything they knew, and it was too large to be a seal.

In February 1980 an almost unique incident occurred when Morgawr may have been seen by someone who was actually looking for it at the time. According to the *Western Morning News* Geoffrey Watson, a sociology student from Thames Polytechnic and a member of the Loch Ness Monster Association, had been staying for a week in Mawnan Smith. One day when he was on patrol on the cliffs near the Helford passage he saw a 'strange dark object' three hundred yards from shore. He managed to take a photograph, but unfortunately when he returned to London and had the film developed it was far too indistinct to make out any definite shape in the water. In fairness to Mr Watson he was dubious about what he had seen; however he was hoping to return to the area in mid-November for another period of sea-watching.

Interestingly, when the report appeared in the *Western Morning News* on 23 February, there was another report in the same paper which talked of massive catches of mackerel and spratt being landed in the Penzance area.

In late 1980 Doc Shiels was filming a television report with the BBC in Cornwall. There were two boats, one with Doc Shiels and friends and the other with the film crew. As they entered the Carrick Roads those in Doc Shiels's boat caught sight of a black hump breaking the surface ahead of them. It was there for only a few seconds and the film crew missed the chance to film it. The following Thursday Doc's daughter Kate claimed to have seen Morgawr just after swimming, naked, in the sea near Pendennis Point. This beast was some three hundred yards offshore and was visible as a hump with a long neck. It was about twenty-five feet long.

The sightings dropped off for a few years until 1985 when Sheila Bird, a Falmouth author, and her brother saw an enormous sea creature on the evening of 10 July. The animal was swimming in Gerrans Bay and approached to within one hundred yards of the witnesses. It was mottled grey in colour with a small, camel-like head on a long neck which projected about five feet above the water surface. Back from the head was an enormous hump. A long tail of indeterminate length streamed out behind.

Two weeks after the sighting by Sheila Bird, but before it became public knowledge, Morgawr was glimpsed again, this time by two visitors from Yorkshire who saw it for about ten seconds before it submerged from Rosemullion Head.

From this point on there has been a tendency to refer to any sea serpent sighting on the south coast of Cornwall, and even west Devon, as Morgawr, instead of restricting the name geographically to the sea serpents of the Helford estuary area.

Typical of these was a report by Nic Johnson published on the *Fortean Times* website. In October 1987 he had been fishing from Devil's Point, a small quay on the Plymouth side of the river Tamar, when a large head popped out of the water ten yards from where he was standing. He described it as like a very large dog in shape, covered with a fur-like green-brown skin, and with forward facing grey eyes which looked directly at him. There were no external ears and the jaws were powerful-looking with a wide mouth. He estimated the size of the animal to be twice that of a horse. He was absolutely certain it was not a seal. The area where he saw it is a channel about 40 metres deep, with strong currents. It is also famous for conger eels, with many record-sized specimens having been taken there.

Whilst reports of strange sea creatures have come sporadically from all over the south Cornish coast, and been referred to as Morgawr, there has also been a continuation of reports from where the original sightings occurred. In September 1995 Gertrude Stevens from Falmouth noticed a strange animal off Rosemullion Head. She reported a dark yellowish-green creature, about twenty feet long, with a small head on the end of a long neck.

There was then a gap of a few years until two sightings were reported in August 1999, both in the Falmouth area, one from a local fisherman and the other from a holidaymaker. In 2000 a television documentary featured two men who said they had made up the whole Morgawr story back in 1975. This statement caused uproar and in the following weeks there was a series of denials and protestations in the local newspapers from some of the early witnesses including George Vinnicombe and Sheila Bird. Some damage was done to the developing legend and to the credibility of past and future witnesses.

In his book, published in 2001, Paul Harrison states that the accounts of certain named witnesses should be regarded as 'complete fabrications'.

The problem is that if Morgawr was a fabrication then there have been literally hundreds of people involved in the conspiracy over the years, many of whom never knew each other. In 1976 alone, whilst there may have been a few tall-story-tellers, it seems unlikely that all the witnesses were making up what they had seen. Even accounting for a couple of overactive imaginations there were still in excess of fourteen witnesses in five separate groups, often from different parts of the country, who saw something in the waters around Falmouth.

A twenty-first century sea serpent

The start of the twenty-first century did not seem to affect the reporting of sightings. In May 2000 a couple touring in a caravan saw an animal off the Falmouth coast. It had two humps and a separate neck and head, and an estimated length of fifteen feet. Clearly neither the visitors nor what they saw had heard that the tales of Morgawr were supposed to be fabrications!

In Late June 2002 the *Cornish Guardian* ran a series of pictures which had been extracted from a video recorded in August 1999 in Gerrans Bay, off the Roseland Peninsula (in south Cornwall). The original videotape had been taken by John Holmes, a former member of staff at the Natural History Museum, who had initially kept it to himself because of business commitments and a fear of being ridiculed.

It was looked at by a video expert who confirmed that the film was totally genuine; it was subsequently passed on to Mike Thomas, the then curator of Newquay Zoo and collator of data on the beast of Bodmin, who in turn passed it on to myself, as a zoologist, and my then colleague Paul Crowther, as an expert on photograph interpretation.

From the outset John Holmes thought it was a 'serpent-like' animal with a small reptilian head. He suggested it could have been a plesiosaur, an aquatic reptile that is generally considered to have become extinct at the same time as the dinosaurs, about sixty-five million years ago. He had estimated its size to be around 2.2 metres long, with the head raised about a metre above the sea surface. This size is below that of the average plesiosaur ascertained from fossil remains.

The preliminary evidence came to me as a series of stills, and it was only a few days later that the video appeared. The conclusions Paul and I came to changed as a result of this. When we first saw the stills, although the shape was possibly that of the plesiosaur (with a small part of the body – the neck and head – above the sea surface), we thought it was probably a sun fish. The sun fish (*Mola mola*) is a species from warmer waters, but one that does come up to the Cornish coast during warm summers – in the previous August (2001) over sixty sun fish had been recorded.

The major characteristic of the sun fish is its tendency to swim at the surface, with its dorsal fin projecting clear of the water and the tip flopping over. This dangling fin tip produces a silhouette which is similar to that of a reptilian head on a long neck. Sun fish can grow up to four metres long and up to two tonnes in weight; they also have a leathery skin with no scales, and it's easy to mistake them for something they aren't. As soon as we had passed our opinions on the still pictures to the *Cornish Guardian* and various other local newspapers, the video arrived.

The problem was that the video showed an animal at the surface, which turned quickly in the opposite direction to that in which it was originally moving. There was no detail of its features, just a dark silhouette. It turned without disturbing the water and that concerned me. If the black silhouette was the tip of a dorsal fin, and there was one to two tonnes of fish immediately below the surface, or indeed a large reptilian body, then for the head and exposed neck/body to veer so suddenly there should have been some serious disturbance of the water.

Reluctantly I came to the conclusion that the animal was actually a sea bird, probably either a cormorant or a shag. When I looked again at the stills the *Cornish Guardian* used on 27 June 2002, I wondered how on earth I had thought it was a sun fish in the first place!

However it is sometimes difficult to gauge size when looking an indeterminate distance out to sea if there are no comparable references in your field of vision at the time.

What could they be?

There are a number of possible answers to this question. The only definite one I can give is that there are almost certainly many different types of animal which have been seen. In his 1965 book *In the Wake of the Sea Serpents*, Bernard Heuvelmans, the father of cryptozoology, examined 358 of the more believable reports and broke them down into nine types on the basis of the descriptions. Two of these have been so rarely seen that they can be effectively ignored.

Each of the remaining seven provides a useful starting point, but care must be taken not to distort a local sighting in order to force it into one of these classes and to avoid having to look any further.

The seven types of sea serpent are:

The super-eel: This is a limbless serpent-type animal, almost certainly a fish, possibly just a large (mutant?) conger eel. The animal(s) in the Lannacombe area in 1906, 1912, and 1970-71 could be in this group.

The super-otter: A large long-tailed mammal resembling an otter.

The mer-horse: A seal-like animal with a long neck and a head with large eyes, whiskers and a mane. Some of the sightings of Morgawr are similar to this.

Many-humped: An elongated animal of very great size with a row of humps spaced regularly along its spine. The 1936 sighting at Brixham loosely fits this description.

Many-finned: An elongated sea animal of great size with rows of triangular-shaped fins.

Long-necked: A sea animal of fairly large size, recognised by its long slender neck and (otherwise) seal-like shape. The animal seen near Port Isaac in 1935 could be in this group. Some of the Morgawr sightings are also similar.

Marine saurian: A primitive sea-going crocodile. The animal described by the crew of the U 28 and U 108 would clearly fall within this category, as would the two animals seen at Looe in 1949.

If we apply the Sherlock Holmes school of logic, i.e. when you have eliminated the impossible, whatever remains, however improbable, must be the truth, then the local sightings can be divided into:

(a) Total fiction – attention-seeking persons have made up the stories, either for their own benefit or for some other ulterior motive.

(b) Mistakes – existing species or marine wreckage have been mistaken for unknown animals. Floating soot, already considered in this book, has been mistaken for a sea-serpent. Oar fish (*Regalecus glesne*) have almost certainly caused confusion. These are deep water marine fish with silver bodies and bright red or pink fins – the dorsal fin runs the length of the body. They grow up to eight metres long and, although usually described as tropical, have been caught in British waters. At that length they could easily be confused with the super-eel group of sea serpents.

Basking sharks (*Cetorhinus maximus*), partly because of their size (up to twelve metres long) and a tendency to swim near the surface, close to the coast in warm weather, could easily be mistaken for sea serpents. When at the surface they often have the top of the tail fin, the dorsal fin and the tip of the snout exposed.

Another suggested candidate for misidentification is the giant squid (*Architeuthis* species). The idea is that the animal floats at the surface with one tentacle raised! I have always found this one a bit far fetched...

A personal view is that elderly male grey seals (*Halichoerus grypus*) may have also been mistaken for some types of sea serpents. The reason for this is fairly straightforward – wildlife films, and to some extent zoos, tend to concentrate on the Californian sealion and the fur seals. These are fairly streamlined and sylph-like and move at speed. The grey seal is larger than the common seal (some males grow up to 400 kg in weight), and the elderly ones often have facial disfigurements, acquired with age, that may make them less than seal-like. As mammals, though, they do have hair, including whiskers, and fairly impressive teeth which feature in many of the sea-serpent reports.

(*c*) *Prehistoric survivors* – or at least the descendants of prehistoric animals. The commonest suggestion is that one or two species of plesiosaur have survived, undiscovered to the present day. Plesiosaurs were large reptiles that flourished in the sea when the dinosaurs were living on land. Accordingly they should have become extinct about sixty-five million years ago when the dinosaurs did. However their chances of surviving the event that led to the extinction of the dinosaurs, though slim, are not necessarily totally impossible, because the sea has always been a more stable environment than the land and temperature changes in it occur more slowly.

Plesiosaurs came in two main body shapes – the long-necked plesiosaurs and the short-necked, but faster pliosaurs. The pliosaurs apparently grew to be the larger of the two species, being possibly up to 12 metres long. Certainly there is at least one suggestion of a pliosaur type body having been washed up, dead, on an African beach in the 1980s. As mentioned earlier, the 'dead plesiosaur' dredged up by a Japanese trawler in 1977 was subsequently identified as the partially decomposed remains of a basking shark.

A group of primitive marine crocodiles known as Thalattosuchians which became extinct possibly 100 million years ago also have similarities to some of the sea serpent sightings. Perhaps undiscovered descendants of this group could account for some of them.

Possibly the most convincing, officially extinct, group of animals with great similarities to the sea serpent sightings are the Zeuglodonts – fish-eating, long slim whales that officially died out about 25 million years ago (i.e. they survived the mass extinction that wiped out the dinosaurs, and evolved during the diversification of the mammals). They were probably the most snake-like mammals known to have existed, and their spinal structure suggests they may have swum by vertical undulations of the back-bone. This contrasts to the horizontal or side-to-side flexures performed by aquatic reptiles and fish. Vertical undulations are of course movements described in several of the sea serpent sightings, and explains why the head could have been projected above the surface of the sea.

When considering whether sea serpents are surviving members of long extinct groups of animals it should be borne in mind that most species have a species lifetime. This is normally less than a million years. Evolution moves on and animals change form, often considerably. Thus an animal that was a six-inch long nocturnal insectivorous type of mammal 65 million years ago evolved into the modern human! The amount of change that could occur in 65 million years to the pliosaur body shape, or in 25 million years to the zeuglodont body shape, must therefore be tremendous. Having said that, some animals do remain unaltered for vast periods of time, and the classic example must be the 1.8 metre long ancient fish known as the coelacanth (*Latimeria chalumne*). It was assumed it had been extinct for over 80 million years until it was rediscovered in 1938.

(d) *Some, as yet, undescribed modern species* that has evolved to a totally different form from its original ancestors.

The future

The sightings of sea serpents so far have not suggested either a single species still requiring formal identification or a series of misidentifications. It seems likely that there are actually a number of large marine species still to be identified. This statement might be thought a little ridiculous in the early years of the twenty-first century, but one of the biggest sharks in the world, the megamouth shark (*Megachasma pelagios*), was only discovered in 1976. Since then less than twenty individual specimens have been found. Amusingly one of these was washed up on a South African beach in 2002, and shortly afterwards a doctored picture of it was circulating on the internet with a claim that it was a dead specimen of 'champ', an alleged lake monster from lake Champlain in the United States.

In 1998 Charles Paxton, a fisheries ecologist with the University of St Andrews in Scotland, published a surprising piece of research in the prestigious *Journal of the Marine Biological Association of the United Kingdom*. In it he produced a graph showing the number of open water, large (over 2 metres) animal species newly recorded since 1758. By projecting the graph forwards he came to the conclusion that there were 47 large species still to be discovered and described. He further predicted that this would probably occur at a rate of one species every 5.3 years, and that most of the animals to be described would be whales. As Paxton is keen to point out, though, there is often a long passage of time between discovery and description/recognition of a new species.

At present Paxton's prediction does seem to be coming true. In November 2000 a journal called *Molecular Biology* reported that some North Pacific right whales may in fact be a different species from the right whales elsewhere. Although it is more of a rethink than a major discovery, it has still increased the number of whale species from 79 to 80.

Many people, quite rightly, will say that if there are still large animals to be discovered in the oceans, why, with modern technology now available, have they not been properly recorded and filmed in recent times? Perhaps, however, it this very technology which is preventing the detection of shy marine species. Consider it this way: although the nineteenth century was the period when merchant marine fleets expanded greatly and trade became truly international, most of the vessels were sailing ships, certainly until the latter part of the century. Their speed was restricted and they were often at sea for long periods of time. There was no radar, so a ship's crew were aware of their surroundings and where they were going because they usually had a number of men 'on watch', including an 'officer of the watch' who was in charge.

Modern shipping tends to use radar to detect conflicting traffic, and echo sounders to confirm that the channel is deep enough for the ship

SEA-SERPENT SEEN BY CAPTAIN CRINGLE.

Captain R J Cringle of the SS Umfali *reported this monster on 4 December 1893, south of the Canary Islands. His ship's log entry is reproduced opposite. The ridicule he suffered made him deeply regret ever seeing it*

to pass through. It also travels consistently faster than sailing ships and therefore there is less chance to observe local wildlife, whether of a known or unknown species. Most passengers on liners, if they see anything, will catch sight of either dolphins or seals. Seals are often on nearby rocks as ships come into port, while dolphins seem to like to elicit contact with ships at sea by riding bow waves.

Most importantly, most modern ships have propellers which, through minor imperfections in their surfaces, set up various noises which travel through the water. Echo sounders too produce noise. All these sounds may frighten large sensitive animals, which will then choose to distance themselves. If this argument is accepted, it is not inconceivable that 'sea serpents' may distance themselves from shipping lanes. Even if some were to swim on the surface towards passing ships, reduced crews 'on watch' are unlikely to record any sightings.

On the other hand, with increased leisure time and greater awareness of wildlife, there may now be more people than ever before walking the cliffs and observing the shores and coastal waters. So perhaps an increase in coastal sightings from them can be expected. That is an exciting prospect.

In the words of a 1990s television series 'The truth is out there'!

H.	K.	F.	COURSES.	WINDS.	LEE-WAY.	Devia-tion.	REMARKS.
1	10	5	S46W¼W	S Sr			Monday Dec 4th 1893 A.m.
2	10	5	"	"			2. Light wind & overcast
3	10	5	"	"			
4	10	5	"	"			4. do , — do
5	10	5	"	"			
6	10	5	"	"			Hands employed cleaning paintwork
7	10	5	"	"			varnishing grain work & painting forecastle
8	10	5	"	"			Carpenter fitting Engine Room Store
9	10	5	"	"			
10	10	5	"	"			12. Calm & clear.
11	10	5	"	"			
12	10	5	"	"			Pumps, wells carefully attended

Course	Dist.	Dif. Lat.	Dep.	Lat. by Acct.	Lat. by Obs.	Dif. Long	Long. by Acct.	Long. by Obs.
South	255	32			22 38 54 N	nil.		17.26.00 W
				Barometer. 30.20	Sympiesometer.	Thermometer. 78°	Aneroid.	

1	10	5	"	Calm			P.m.
2	10	5	"	"			2. Calm & smooth sea
3	10	5	"	"			
4	10	5	"	"			4. Same weather. Th 43
5	10	5	"	"			
6	10	5	"	"			5.30 Sighted and passed about 500 yards
7	10	5	"	"			from ship a Monster Fish of the Serpent
8	10	5	"	"			shape, about 80ft-long with slimy skin
9	10	5	"	"			and short-fins at about 20 feet-apart on
10	10	5	"	"			the back & in circ, about the size of a
11	10	5	"	"			full sized Whale, I distinctly saw the fish's
12	10	5	"	"			mouth open & shut with my glasses. It
							Jaws appeared to me about 7 feet long
							with large teeth, In shape it was

Just like a Conger Eel, There were two of them ...

Master _____ _____ Mate

Further reading

This needs to be considered in two sections: the records from the past
and where to look for news now and in the future. The classic reports
of sea serpents and similar entities are spread across many text books
and other forms of media, some of which are listed below. The most
direct reports of sightings tend to appear in the media of the day. For
example, the original reports of the *Daedalus* sighting can be found in
The Times – many large reference libraries keep a full set of *The Times*

on microfilm. The *Falmouth Packet* has, in recent times, almost been a clearing house for sightings of Morgawr.

Reports of findings in the future are likely to be recorded in a variety of media. Most large new species will be mentioned in the *Fortean Times*, the monthly journal of strange phenomena, shortly after they are formally described in the scientific journals. Similarly the Exeter-based Centre for Fortean Zoology produce a magazine called *Animals and Men* which also lists new species when they are described. More detailed reports can usually be found by using search engines on the internet with search phrases such as 'newly described species', 'new marine species', etc.

Classic sea serpent references

Bord, J and Bord, C, *Modern Mysteries of Britain* (Guild Publishing, Guildford, 1987)

Bright, M, *There are Giants in the Sea* (Robson Books, London, 1989)

Clarke, D, 'The Myth and Mystery of Morgawr the Helford Monster' (*Cornish Life*, Vol. 4, No. 4, 1977)

Downes, J, *The Owl Man and Others* (Centre for Fortean Zoology, Exeter, 2002)

Harrison, P, *Sea Serpents and Lake Monsters of the British Isles* (Robert Hale, London, 2001)

Heuvelmans, B, *In the Wake of the Sea-serpents* (Rupert Hart-Davis, London, 1968)

Heuvelmans, B, *The Kraken and the Colossal Octopus* (Kegan-Paul, London, 1968)

Mawnan-Peller, A, *Morgawr – the Monster of Falmouth Bay* (Centre for Fortean Zoology, Exeter, 1996. This book was originally published in 1976)

Oudemans, A C, *The Great Sea-Serpent* (Luzac and Co., London, 1892)

Rawlings, E, 'Morgawr – Serpent of the Cornish Shores' (*Cornwall Today*, September 2001, pages 74-78)

Shuker, Karl, *In search of Prehistoric Survivors* (Blandford, London, 1995)